NORTH KENT TRAMWAYS

Robert J Harley

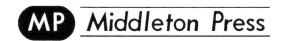

MP Middleton Press

First published December 1994

ISBN 1 873793 44 8

© Middleton Press 1994

Design - Deborah Goodridge

Published by Middleton Press
                    Easebourne Lane
                    Midhurst
                    West Sussex
                    GU29 9AZ
                    Tel: (0730) 813169
(From 16 April 1995 - (01730) 813169)

Printed & bound by Biddles Ltd,
                    Guildford and Kings Lynn

CONTENTS

Woolwich to Dartford   1
Gravesend Tramways   60
Sheerness Tramways   96
Herne Bay Pier   119

1 Woolwich to Dartford
Woolwich and Plumstead   1
Abbey Wood and Erith   13
Bexleyheath and Welling   29
Dartford and Horns Cross   46
Joyce Green Hospital   57

2 Gravesend Tramways
Northfleet   60
Gravesend   68
Rolling Stock   87

3 Sheerness Tramways
Sheerness   96
Rolling Stock   117

4 Herne Bay Pier
Herne Bay Pier   119

INTRODUCTION AND ACKNOWLEDGEMENTS

This volume sets out to describe the tramways of Gravesend and Sheerness which have not been covered previously in the Tramway Classics series. As an introduction to the area, the reader is treated to a tramride between Woolwich and Dartford, Horns Cross. Those who have read the companion Middleton Press volume *Greenwich and Dartford Tramways* will already be familiar with this journey. However, this time there are new sights to see along the way. The earlier book also contains much historical information on the Bexley, Erith and Dartford tramways and readers are directed to this volume for added background material.

Many of the views which are included in this present work come from the collection of the late Alan Watkins and I offer my thanks to Ann Watkins for permission to use them. I knew Alan for 20 years and he was always willing to share his enthusiasm for the tramways he rode on as a child. He often gave lectures at local history gatherings throughout Kent and South East London, and thanks to his scholarship much valuable material was saved for posterity. I am certain he would have acknowledged the selection of street scenes which fill the following pages as a fitting tribute to a means of transport which served the public so well for many years. I very much appreciate the help given by all those who have contributed photographs to illustrate this book, in particular I would like to thank Richard Rosa of Gravesend who has made available many rarities from his splendid collection of historic postcards. My thanks also go to Godfrey Croughton and Graham Page for copies of their tickets.

1. Woolwich to Dartford

WOOLWICH AND PLUMSTEAD

1. Bexley Council Tramways car 22 waits to take on passengers at Beresford Square, Woolwich; the journey out to Horns Cross, Dartford will take about 75 minutes and the return fare is a modest one shilling (5p)! (G.N.Southerden)

2. In this Edwardian scene two horse trams pass outside the gate to Woolwich Arsenal. The London terminus for these narrow gauge (3ft. 6ins./1067mm) cars had been at Tunnel Avenue since June 1906. Subsequently the LCC electrified the whole line and converted the track gauge to standard. (J.B.Gent Coll.)

3. In August 1944 London Transport installed a new curve in Beresford Square and as can be seen in this 1979 view, this trackwork outlived the rest of the system by many years. Notice the pattern of the blue-grey granite setts, so typical of the tramway era. (R.J.Harley)

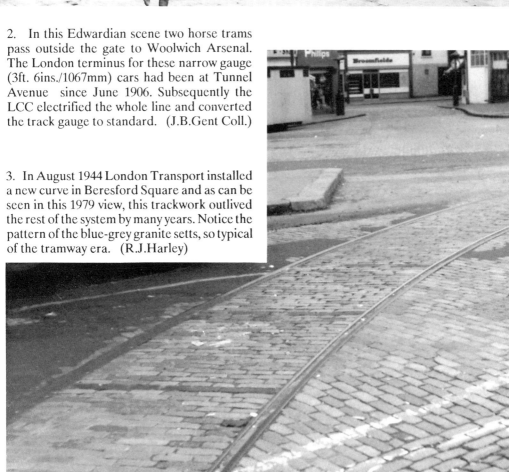

4. Beresford Square is also the location for Woolwich market and electric cars reached here in April 1908. Next to LCC car 118 is the market inspectors' hut with the rules and regulations pasted on the front. (J.B.Gent Coll.)

D 2246		
Bexley Council Tramways and Dartford Light Railways.		
Beresford Square	1d	Horn's Cross
Plumstead Station	1/2	Bleakar Loop
Plumstead Corner		Milestone Road
King's High way		Park Road
Wickham Church		Bull Hotel
Foster's Schools		West Hill Schools
Nag's Head		Maiden Lane
Danson Road		Crayford Bridge
Lion Road		Elm Loop
Market Place		Pinnacle Hill

Kh 1507		
DOWN	1d	UP
Plumstead Church		Market Place
King's Highway		Upton Road
Foresters		Nag's
Duchess		Duchess
Nag's Head		Foresters
Upton Rd		King's Highway
Market Place		Kashgar Road
Barne- house		Plumstead Station
Northum- berl'ndHch		Beresford Square
Employees		Employees

D 7245		
Bexley Council Tramways and Dartford Light Railways		
Beresford Square	2d	Horn's Cross
Plumstead Station		Breaker Loop
Plumstead Corner		Milestone Road
King's Highway		Park Road
Wickham Church		Bull Hotel
Foster's Schools		West Hill Schools
Nag's Head		Maldon Lane
Danson Road		Crayford Bridge
Lion Road		Elm Loop
Market Place		Pinnacle Hill

Eb 5719		
Bexley Council Tramways and Dartford Light Railways		
Beresford Square	2d	Horn's Cross
Plumstead Station		Breaker Loop
Plumstead Corner		Milestone Road
King's Highway		Park Road
Wickham Church		Bull Hotel
Foster's Schools		West Hill Schools
Nag's Head		Maldon Lane
Danson Road		Crayford Bridge
Lion Road		Elm Loop
Market Place		Pinnacle Hill

5. We now set off on the road to North Kent in company with Bexley car 5 which still bears its original oil lamp on the dash. The tram is passing the entrance to Griffin Road, Plumstead and will shortly enter a section of single track with passing loops along Plumstead High Street. (R.Rosa Coll.)

6. Just off Lakedale Road the first electric trams were kept in the former horse tram depot until the new car sheds at Abbey Wood opened in April 1910. Car 178 is pictured early in its life; a similar vehicle has been preserved in operating condition at the National Tramway Museum in Crich, Derbyshire. (R.J.Harley Coll.)

7. Further along the High Street, Bexley car 16 waits for an oncoming tram to clear the single track before going on its way. (R.Rosa Coll.)

8. The junction of Wickham Lane and Bostall Hill was the parting of the ways for the Bexley trams and the LCC services to Abbey Wood. Here we observe a brand new LCC car from the 552-601 batch of trams which had new bodies fitted to trucks and electrical equipment from withdrawn single deck F and G class cars. (R.Elliott)

9. A short distance from the previous view car 306 stops at the passing loop opposite Woodhurst Road. This view dates from the early 1950s, not long before the final abandonment of trams in July 1952. (C.Carter)

10. A tram swings into Basildon Road after having negotiated the points in the foreground. In the distance a bus on route 99 tackles the grade of Bostall Hill. (John C.Gillham)

11. Car 93 has just climbed the slope in Basildon Road and the motorman is about to ease his charge across the road junction into Bostall Hill. Only one motor car spoils an otherwise traffic free view; note that the tramway and trolleybus overhead wires are separate on this stretch. (D.A.Thompson)

12. At the foot of Basildon Road on 24th July 1916 an LCC tramcar derailed on the bend leading to McLeod Road and overturned. A crowd has gathered to survey the damage whilst motor lorry 25 in the LCC service fleet waits to salvage electrical equipment from the stricken car. In order to prevent any future tram taking the curve at high speed a compulsory stop was later installed on the corner of McLeod Road. (R.Rosa Coll.)

13. A splendid array of electric street traction greets the visitor to Abbey Wood on this summer's day in 1952. After the demise of the trams, trolleybus route 698 soldiered on for another seven years until it too was swept aside by diesel buses in March 1959. We are left to wonder why large amounts of money were spent by London Transport ridding the capital of an efficient, environmentally friendly transport system, when many other European countries were modernising and upgrading their tramways. (C.Carter)

14. The terminus of Erith Council Tramways in Abbey Road was just round the corner from the LCC tracks in Knee Hill. Unfortunately through services were never operated from Erith into London, thus car 9 was fated to spend its days shuttling between Abbey Wood and Bexleyheath. Note the driver swinging the trolley whilst the conductor helps passengers alight on this March day in 1928. Near this spot today an unsightly flyover has completely changed the view towards Erith. (G.N.Southerden)

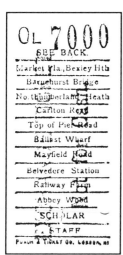

15. The crew of Erith car 3 pose for the photographer as the sunshine strikes the shop blinds on the corner of Station Road, Abbey Wood. Although only a few passengers are evident, the tram will gradually fill up as it journeys through Belvedere to Erith town centre. (H.A.Whitcombe)

16. The Abbey Wood to Northend service lasted from 26th August to 18th September 1905. In this rare view car 2, in its original apple green and primrose livery, is observed in West Street at the level crossing with several industrial railway lines. This is beyond the signal box on the right. There seems to be some jostling for position amongst the carters following the tram; a venerable gentleman gazes at the new transport wonder of the age. (R.Rosa Coll.)

17. Further along West Street where it joins Walnut Tree Road, a set of three standard gauge railway tracks was crossed on the level. An Erith bogie car, one of the batch acquired from the London United Tramways in 1915, is about to swing round the curve on its way to Abbey Wood. (G.N.Southerden)

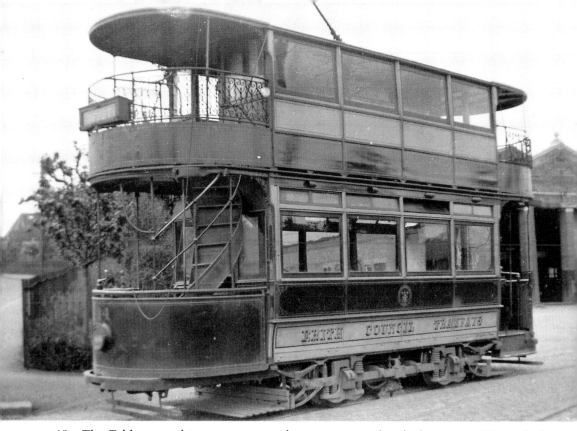

18. The Erith covered top cars were quite substantial vehicles and they lasted into the London Transport era. Behind car 14 is the depot which was closed on 28th December 1933; the remaining trams needed for the line were moved to the larger ex-LCC car sheds at Abbey Wood. The Erith depot was preserved for many years with tram tracks intact until "progress" in the form of 1970s town planners caught up with it! (R.Elliott)

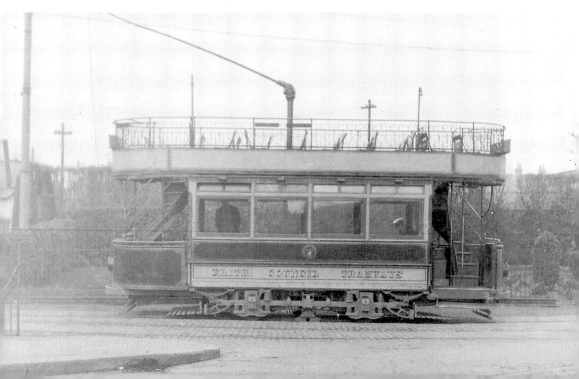

19. On one of the depot approach tracks we get a fine broadside view of an Erith open top car. Not long after this shot was taken, the new owners, London Transport, instigated a last round up of antiquated trams and the car pictured here was towed off into the sunset. (G.N.Southerden)

20. Car 19, seen outside the depot, was a very solid looking vehicle christened the "tank" by the crews. Its home town was Kingston-upon-Hull and it sailed into the Thames in 1916 on a barge supplied by the Yorkshire port. After unloading it was employed in shifting the large crowds of munitions workers vital for the war effort; later it met the same fate as many of its stable mates, and it was scrapped by LT in 1933. (G.N.Southerden)

21. A final look at the depot on a gloomy March day in 1928 as one of the ex-LUT cars is prepared for service. These vehicles were rebuilt by Erith Council Tramways in 1922 to incorporate direct stairs and an extended top deck canopy over the driving platforms. (G.N.Southerden)

22. A brighter day in Walnut Tree Road and car 4 halts just short of the depot entrance on a training run before the official opening of the tramways in 1905. (R.J.Harley Coll.)

23. We are standing at the Wheatley Hotel junction in the late 1920s. Car 17, with the conductor collecting the fares on the top deck, has just climbed Walnut Tree Road. The motorman at the controls holds the car on the handbrake long enough for the photographer to compose his picture, unfortunately the impatient cyclist was not troubled by such considerations. (H.A.Whitcombe)

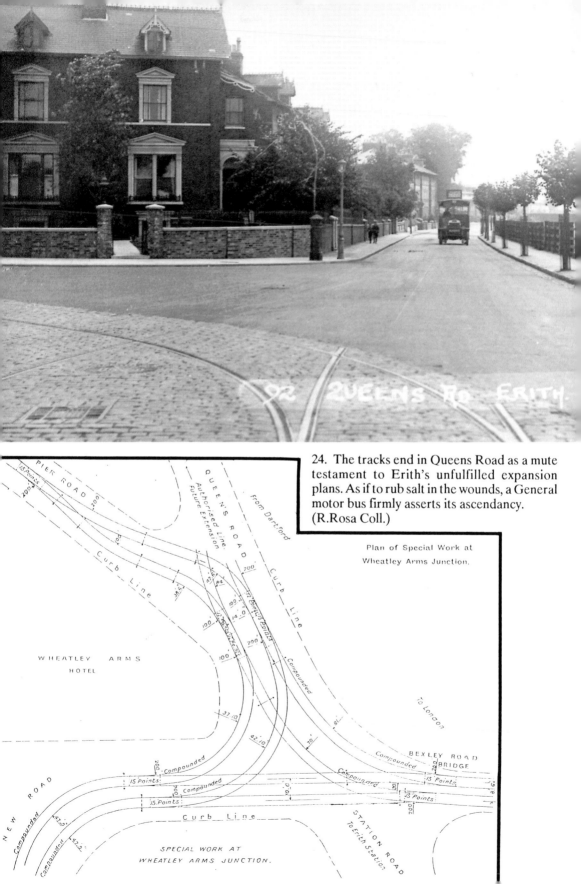

24. The tracks end in Queens Road as a mute testament to Erith's unfulfilled expansion plans. As if to rub salt in the wounds, a General motor bus firmly asserts its ascendancy. (R.Rosa Coll.)

Plan of Special Work at Wheatley Arms Junction.

PIER ROAD

QUEENS ROAD

From Dartford

Authorised Line. Future Extension.

15 Points.

200

200

200

100

100

100

100

200

14.0

200

37.0

42.10

70

8

To London

Curb Line

Curb Line

Compounded

WHEATLEY ARMS HOTEL

BEXLEY ROAD BRIDGE

Compounded

15 Points.

NEW ROAD

Compounded

15 Points.

Compounded

15 Points.

Compounded

Compounded

15 Points.

3 Points.

STATION ROAD

To Erith Station

Curb Line

SPECIAL WORK AT WHEATLEY ARMS JUNCTION.

25. Car 9 is pictured in Pier Road in 1905; at that time the buildings in central Erith were on a more human scale. Extensive redevelopment in the 1970s and 1980s has changed so much that it is often impossible to locate street patterns of years gone by. (R.Rosa Coll.)

In connection with London Transport's programme for substituting trolleybuses for trams on 148 miles of route, the tram routes set out below will be converted to trolleybus routes on the dates shown

Date	Tram Route		Trolleybus Route
Nov. 10	40	Section WOOLWICH (Beresford Square) and ABBEY WOOD	698	WOOLWICH (Free Ferry) Erith and BEXLEYHEATH Every 7 minutes
	98	ABBEY WOOD Erith and BEXLEYHEATH		
During Nov.	96	WOOLWICH (Beresford Square) Welling and HORNS CROSS	696	WOOLWICH (Free Ferry) Welling and DARTFORD (Market Street) Every 4 minutes to Bexleyheath Every 7 minutes to Dartford

Note: The tram track between Dartford and Horns Cross will be abandoned. A cheap return fare for workmen will be available on the frequent service of motor buses operating over the section of the tramway to be abandoned.

Tram Routes 36 and 38 will continue to operate between Abbey Wood, Woolwich, and Victoria Embankment.

TIMES of first and last trolleybuses are shown overleaf.

26. A world away from the busy metropolis with its smoke and grime is this section of Bexley Road, Erith depicted in the first decade of the twentieth century. What a ride it must have been, sitting on the open balcony of the approaching tramcar, which gave a grandstand view of the passing trees and the rural landscape. (R.Rosa Coll.)

27. In the summer of 1935 work got under way to erect the overhead needed for the replacing trolleybuses on route 698 which took over on 10th November 1935. One of the new trolleybus fittings can be seen next to the two tram wires in this photo. Even though the end was near, car 1698 still looks smartly turned out as it rocks and sways over the worn rails in Bexley Road. (D.W.K.Jones)

28. In the days before through working commenced in July 1908, an Erith car rests just yards away from Bexley Council track at Northumberland Heath. (R.Rosa Coll.)

29. We now change trams to a Bexley vehicle, which differs from its Erith counterpart in that it is painted maroon red and cream, and it possesses reversed stairs. The Bexley livery subsequently weathered to a dark chocolate colour. (John H.Meredith Coll.)

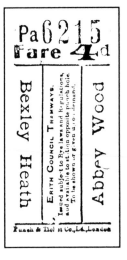

30. Indeed there were some splendid sights to be seen in Kentish lanes during Edwardian times, as car 8 proves when it makes a photo stop in the middle of the countryside. (R.J.Harley Coll.)

31. Trackwork is in progress and the permanent way department flat truck has been hitched to passenger car 11. In this early winter scene the exhaust from a steam lorry drifts across the background. Alas all too soon the rolling hills and fields will be covered by 1930s housing estates and this rural tramway will be gone for ever. (G.N.Southerden)

32. In 1928 there was a marked lack of motor traffic at Bexleyheath Clock Tower, which was journey's end for the Erith open top tram on the left of the picture. On the main line two covered top Bexley cars pass at the loop opposite Penney, Son & Parker Ltd. (G.N.Southerden)

33. A closer look at the Bexleyheath terminus with an Erith eight wheel car pictured just after the formation of London Transport in July 1933. The letter D after the fleet number was applied by the new owners; this tram was not later renumbered or repainted in standard LT red and cream. (G.N.Southerden)

34. The state of the pointwork in Bexleyheath Broadway tells its own story; it is hardly surprising that replacement of the trams in this area was such a high priority for London Transport. On the left of the Clock Tower a domed roof ex-East Ham car has taken over the Bexleyheath to Abbey Wood service, now LT route 98. On the right two ex-LCC M class are working between Woolwich and Horns Cross on LT route 96.   (A.J.Watkins Coll.)

35.   Passengers run for shelter as another summer shower is in the offing. The conductor of the short working Bexley car is swinging the trolley pole ready for the return trip to Woolwich. All this activity has been frozen in time in this pre-First World War scene. (R.Rosa Coll.)

36. The BP petrol pumps behind car 4 indicate that the motoring age has started to make an impact on everyday life. However, the trams still have plenty of customers, as the number of British households possessing a motor car was still quite small in 1928 when this photograph was taken.   (G.N.Southerden)

DINE AT
MUNICIPAL RESTAURANT
Xn 5315
FARE 1½d

Market Place Bexley Heath		Carlton Road
Barneh'rst Bridge		Top of Pier Road
Northumberland Heath		Ballast Wharf
Carlton Road		Mayfield Road
Top of Pier Road		Belvedere Station
Ballast Wharf		Railway Farm
Mayfield Road		Abbey Wood Station

Punch & Ticket Co. Ld., London

→

37. A.Hide & Co, the Cash Drapers have their sale on as car 26C draws to a halt on the passing loop outside. This is the first summer of London Transport operation and soon this tram will be making the one way trip to the scrapyard. (G.N.Southerden)

38. On 24th November 1935 trolleybus route 696 replaced tram service 96 to Dartford; car 1691 waits at Bexleyheath just before the fateful day. Trolleybus route 696 was itself replaced by diesel buses on 3rd March 1959, and the new vehicles bore the route number 96....Plus ca change! (R.J.Harley Coll.)

VI. The speed at which the carriages shall be driven or propelled along the tramways shall not exceed the rate of—

Ten miles an hour—
  (a.) In Erith Road between the railway bridge and May Place Road.
  (b.) In the Broadway and Dover Road between Erith Road and a marked pole at the east end of the village of Welling.
  (c.) In Wickham Lane between the Dover Road and Wickham Church gateway.
  (d.) In Wickham Lane and High Street, Plumstead, between the termination of the double line at the bottom of Wickham Hill and the terminus of the line in Plumstead.

Six miles an hour—
  In May Place Road between Erith Road and the market place.

Four miles an hour—
  (a.) Through facing points, whether fixed or movable.
  (b.) In Erith Road, from the terminus at Northumberland Heath to Courtleet Bottom, on the inward journey.
  (c.) In Erith Road, from the railway bridge to Courtleet Bottom, on the outward journey.
  (d.) On the curve between the Broadway and May Place Road.
  (e.) In Wickham Lane, from the Wickham Church gateway to the termination of the double line at the bottom of Wickham Hill, on the descending journey.
  (f.) On the curve between Wickham Lane and High Street, Plumstead.

At all other places the speed shall not exceed the rate of *eight* miles an hour.

39. In contrast to the sorry state of the system in its latter days, this 1903 scene demonstrates why all eyes were on the brand new electrical marvel which could offer a frequent and cheap public service. In addition car 1 could easily outpace the rest of the horse drawn traffic, examples of which are seen here in Bexleyheath Broadway. (R.J.Harley Coll.)

40. Several miles west of Bexleyheath along the line of the ancient Watling Street lies Welling. Outside the Nags Head car 16 enters the passing loop.The section of single track was protected by the semaphore signal attached to the bracket arm on the right of the tram. (R.Rosa Coll.)

41. In the foreground the siding at Welling Corner can just be discerned. A crowd has gathered to witness the plight of car 8 which has just derailed; the tram behind is working a temporary shuttle service from Welling to Woolwich. (R.Rosa Coll.)

42. We have come full circle with this view of Bexley car 4 at the junction previously illustrated in picture 8. Although this section of track in Wickham Lane lay in the County of London, the LCC showed no inclination to run a regular service. Briefly around 1913/15 the LCC extended service 38 on Sundays only to Bexleyheath Broadway, but afterwards they were quite happy to let the Bexley four wheel cars have the road to themselves. (H.A.Whitcombe)

43. We return to Bexley tram depot sometime around opening day in 1903. Note the sparkling condition of the tram which has yet to be fitted with its wire mesh lifeguards. (R.J.Harley Coll.)

44. One wonders whether the official photographer did in fact ask this rather glum group to smile for the camera! Perhaps it was not good form in those days to grin on these occasions. Some of the men pictured here fell in action during the First World War. (R.J.Harley Coll.)

45. The coming of electric tramways aroused much public interest around the turn of the century. The flags are out at the Prince Albert on the corner of Gravel Hill, where the new Dartford Council Tramways single track is about to be connected to the existing Bexley lines. In 1905 this event was viewed as another indication of progress towards greater local prosperity. (A.J.Watkins Coll.)

DARTFORD AND HORNS CROSS

46. The chap on the left strolling along London Road, Crayford glances across at the painter busily at work on the front railings; a Dartford tramcar clatters over the points outside Lyle & Sons, Mineral Water Manufacturers in this view taken around 1907. (R.Rosa Coll.)

47. Deeper into Dartford territory we pass West Hill Schools. Car 9 waits for another tram coming from behind the photographer before it begins the descent into Dartford town centre. (E.C.Youens)

48. Opposite the Bull Hotel in Dartford High Street, the motorman of car 1693 shuts off power as he coasts over the junction with the lines to Hythe Street. Several crew men were transferred into the district by London Transport around 1934 when this photo was taken. So the story goes, a conductor returned to Abbey Wood depot to be told that a motorman with whom he used to work, had been "sent to Bexley." Somewhat taken aback, the conductor replied that he always thought that particular driver was too highly strung. Much hilarity ensued especially when the motorman at Bexley depot got to hear of the incident. South East Londoners know that for many unfortunates the phrase "sent to Bexley" means enforced incarceration in the large LCC mental institution situated just outside the town! (A.B.Cross Coll.)

49. Flags, bunting, garlands of flowers and coloured lights festoon car 12 which is decorated for the coronation of King George V on 22nd June 1911. (C.Carter Coll.)

50. More decorated trams, this time the celebrations were for the official opening ceremony performed on 14th February 1906; no doubt, one of the speeches in the reception afterwards would have wished success and good fortune to the new enterprise. Unfortunately, the splendid vehicles seen here only lasted eleven years as the depot and all the tramcars were consumed in a disasterous fire in August 1917. Bexley came to the rescue and maintained the service with help from the LCC who loaned some B class cars which were surplus to their requirements. (R.Rosa Coll.)

51. The Wilmington branch was never very profitable and it was normally worked by a single shuttle car which plied the route from Dartford station to the terminus outside the Co-op, Wilmington seen here on the right. (G.N.Southerden)

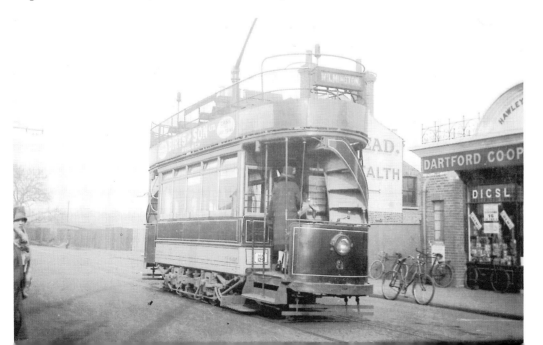

52. A last look at Wilmington terminus with car 1 photographed about 1930. It did not take long for London Transport to axe the line and the last car ran on 17th April 1934. (E.C.Youens)

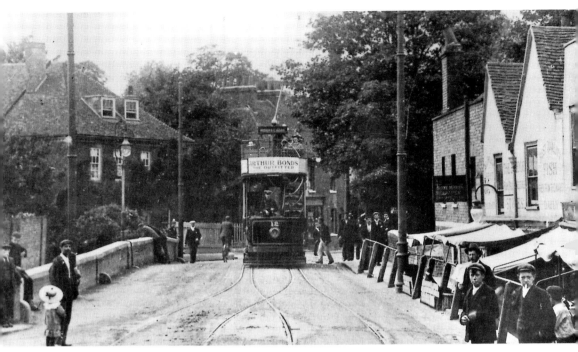

53. We now set off again in the direction of Horns Cross and Gravesend. Car 12 is in Overy Liberty, Dartford; note the interlaced track on the bridge over the River Darent. (R.J.Harley Coll.)

54. The climb out of town begins with East Hill; this was the scene of an accident on 5th February 1919 when LCC car 131, on loan to Bexley, got out of control on the gradient, derailed at the bridge and collided with a tree. According to the inspecting officer's report.."the accident was fortunately not attended by any serious results, two passengers only having complained of shock and the driver being uninjured..the woodwork of the front platform was considerably damaged, and the hand-brake gear injured." (R.Rosa Coll.)

55. On the way to Horns Cross near Bow Arrow Hospital, a covered top car is glimpsed in the distance. The undulating nature of the landscape is apparent and the tall chimney is evidence of the extensive industrial presence in this area which has been associated with the production of cement for many years. (J.H.Meredith Coll.)

56. The track and overhead ceased at Horns Cross by the Bull public house. The road continues past car 30 and in a couple of miles the terminus of the Gravesend system will be reached. The vital track connection was never made, thus leaving the field clear for the motor bus to provide the useful through service between Dartford and Gravesend. (G.N.Southerden)

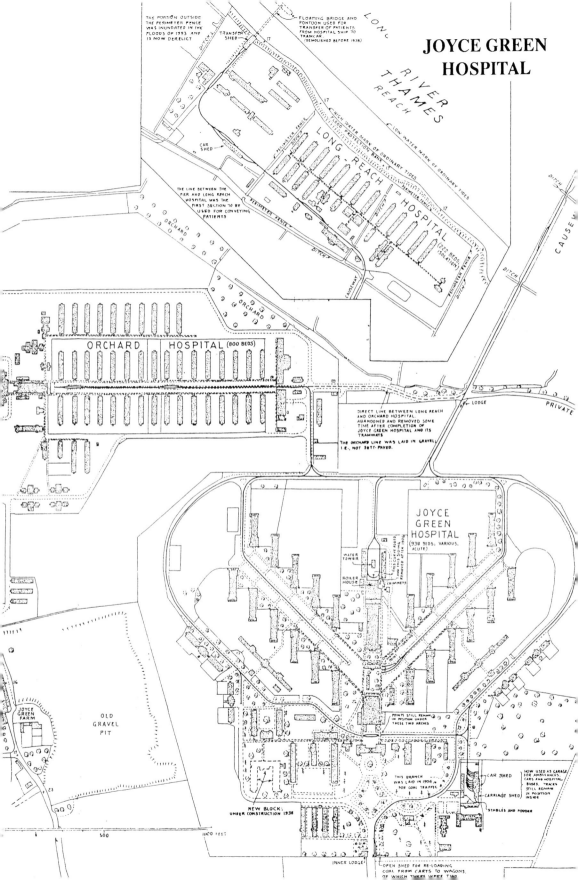

JOYCE GREEN HOSPITAL

THE PORTION OUTSIDE THE PERIMETER FENCE WAS INUNDATED IN THE FLOODS OF 1953 AND IS NOW DERELICT

FLOATING BRIDGE AND PONTOON USED FOR TRANSFER OF PATIENTS FROM HOSPITAL SHIP TO TRAMCAR. (DEMOLISHED BEFORE 1938)

TRANSFER SHED

CAR SHED

THE LINE BETWEEN THE PIER AND LONG REACH HOSPITAL WAS THE FIRST SECTION TO BE USED FOR CONVEYING PATIENTS

RIVER THAMES
LONG REACH

HIGH WATER MARK OF ORDINARY TIDES
LOW WATER MARK OF ORDINARY TIDES

FLOOD PROTECTION BANK
PERIMETER FENCE

LONG-REACH HOSPITAL
(223 BEDS, ISOLATION)

CAUSEWAY
DITCH
CAUSEWAY

PRIVATE

ORCHARD HOSPITAL (800 BEDS)

DIRECT LINE BETWEEN LONG REACH AND ORCHARD HOSPITAL. ABANDONED AND REMOVED SOME TIME AFTER COMPLETION OF JOYCE GREEN HOSPITAL AND ITS TRAMWAYS.

THE ORCHARD LINE WAS LAID IN GRAVEL I.E., NOT SETT-PAVED.

LODGE

JOYCE GREEN HOSPITAL
(938 BEDS, VARIOUS, ACUTE)

WATER TOWER

BOILER HOUSE
CHIMNEYS

THIS CURVE WAS REMOVED AFTER 1930

POINTS STILL REMAIN IN POSITION UNDER THESE TWO ARCHES

JOYCE GREEN FARM

OLD GRAVEL PIT

THIS BRANCH WAS LAID IN 1904 FOR COAL TRAFFIC

NEW BLOCK, UNDER CONSTRUCTION 1938

CAR SHED

CARRIAGE SHED

STABLES AND POUND

NOW USED AS GARAGE FOR AMBULANCES, CARS AND HOSPITAL BUSES. TRACKS STILL REMAIN IN POSITION INSIDE

INNER LODGE

OPEN SHED FOR RE-LOADING COAL FROM CARTS TO WAGONS, OF WHICH THERE WERE TWO

500   1000 FEET

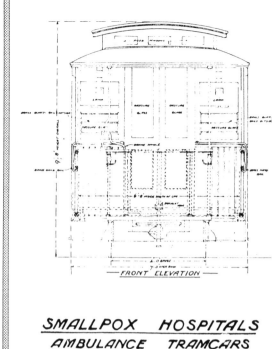

SMALLPOX HOSPITALS AMBULANCE TRAMCARS

FRONT ELEVATION

57. Horse tramways on a gauge of 4ft./1219mm were opened in May 1897 at the Joyce Green Hospital site north of Dartford. They eventually also connected Long Reach and Orchard hospitals; the cars pictured here at the depot were delivered in 1905/8 and, as the accompanying plan shows, each vehicle was equipped with beds and a heating system to aid the care of patients as they were moved around the medical complex. (J.H.Price Coll.)

58. The rails of the tramway stand idle at Orchard Hospital as members of "the other ranks" take a welcome convalescent break from the horrors of the First World War. (J.H.Price Coll.)

59. Equine motive power was dispensed with around 1925 and the trams were then hauled by Talbot motor ambulances. Here a patient has just been carried out of the tram and an attendant returns to pick up the boarding plank and stow it back on the car. (J.H.Price Coll.)

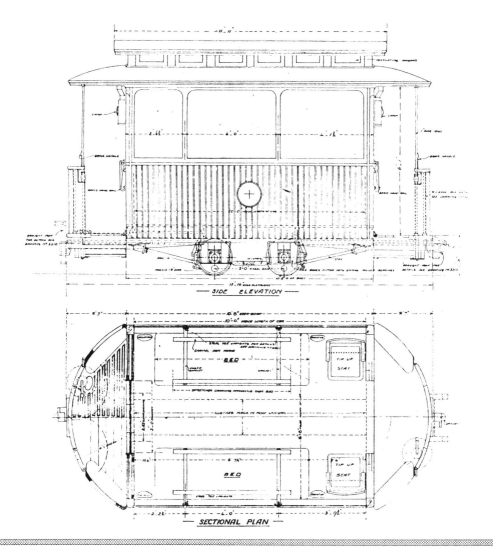

— SIDE ELEVATION —

— Sectional Plan —

2. Gravesend Tramways

CONTENTS

6	Northfleet	60
7	Gravesend	69
8	Rolling Stock	87

GEOGRAPHICAL SETTING

The countryside around Gravesend and Northfleet is one of chalk hills and dry valleys. In places the land rises steeply from the banks of the River Thames and many parts, particularly in Northfleet and Swanscombe, have been scarred by quarrying and other industrial processes used in connection with the cement industry. The southern approaches to Gravesend are on the slope of the North Downs which still contain areas of unspoilt natural beauty.

The plans used in this section come from the Ordnance Survey 1909 edition and are to a scale of 25" to one mile (1:2500).

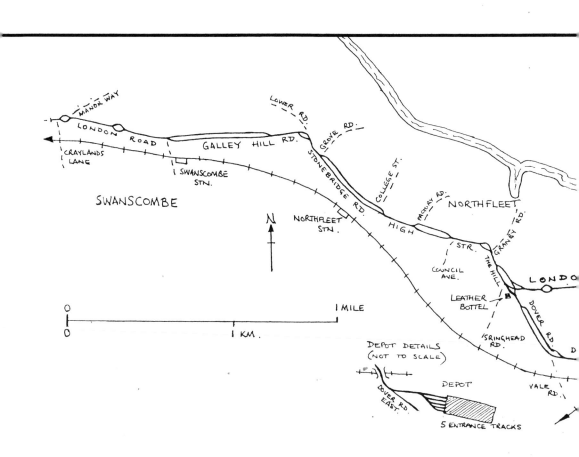

HISTORICAL BACKGROUND

Much of the early history of this area centres on the River Thames which forms a natural highway for trade and commerce. Gravesham as a settlement is mentioned in the Domesday Book and the modern town of Gravesend grew up as a pilot station and customs post for the Port of London. The town was incorporated by charter in the reign of Queen Elizabeth I in 1567/8. The nineteenth century saw the arrival of the first railway in 1845 with a line to Strood; the more important section westwards to the capital opened in 1849. Full details of the intricate local railway history will be had by reading the Middleton Press album *Dartford to Sittingbourne*.

Further rail traction reached the town in the shape of narrow gauge horse trams which opened on a route between the centre of Gravesend and the Leather Bottel, Northfleet in June 1883. An extension along The Hill and Northfleet High Street was inaugurated by electric traction in April 1889, thus making Northfleet a pioneer in local transport. Unfortunately, as with many early electrical installations, the system was never regarded as more than an experiment and the faithful horse took over in November 1890.

After this one false start, a permanent electric tramway system was proposed by the British Electric Traction Company. The horse cars finished on 30th June 1901, the tracks were reconstructed to standard gauge and the following services were opened:

Leather Bottel to Gravesend Clock Tower on 2nd August 1902.
Extensions to Denton, Swanscombe and along Pelham Road on 22nd September 1903.
Along Dover Road to join the Pelham Road line on 30th January 1903.
Along Windmill Street to the Old Prince of Orange public house on 4th December 1903.

The services offered by the new enterprise, called the Gravesend and Northfleet Electric Tramways Ltd., comprised a main line route from Denton to Swanscombe and branch services from Gravesend town centre to the Pelham Arms and along Windmill Street to the Old Prince of Orange. Trams also worked along Dover Road from the Leather Bottel to

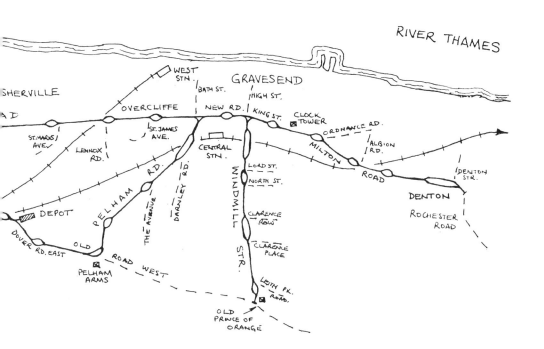

the Pelham Arms, but it soon became apparent that this section lacked patronage and it became very much the "lame duck" of the company. The company also seems to have got its sums wrong as to the number and type of tramcars that were needed, and the large eight wheel cars, that the company had originally ordered, had all been sold to other operators in the BET organization by 1906. Economies were made by buying two small single deck demi cars, each operated by one man, which were used on the Windmill Street and Dover Road lines. In 1915 double deck cars reappeared on Windmill Street and both demi cars were then left to wear out, working from the Leather Bottel along Dover Road. In 1921 two replacement single deck cars were purchased from the recently defunct Taunton system. However, although a new brighter livery was adopted in the 1920s and some trams had top covers fitted, the writing was on the wall for the single track and loop tramways which could not compete with the new motor buses. The end came on 28th February 1929 when Maidstone and District Motor Services vehicles replaced the trams.

NORTHFLEET

How the contemporary technical press saw Northfleet's bold experiment.
An extract from "Engineering" of 15th March 1889.

THE SERIES ELECTRICAL TRAMWAY SYSTEM.

DURING three days of the present week the Series Electrical Traction Syndicate, Limited, of 11, Queen Victoria-street, E.C., have been showing their new tramway at Northfleet, Kent, to gentlemen interested in such questions. The tramway is three-quarters of a mile in length, and forms part of an extended system connecting Northfleet and Gravesend. The whole can be traversed by horse cars, but the part mentioned can also be worked by electricity, and two cars will begin to run upon it regularly next Monday. Although this piece of line has been laid down for purposes of demonstration, yet it is not in any sense tentative. All the arrangements are as permanent as those of the best horse lines of the kingdom, and the cars have been specially built for the occasion. We have so recently described the mechanical and electrical features of the series system of traction (see page 139 *ante*), that it is not necessary to repeat them, further than to explain that the motors of all the cars on the line are in series, the current going through each of them in succession. The current is conveyed to the cars through an insulated cable carried underground in a closed tube, and having contact pieces or "spring jacks" placed 21 ft. apart in a conduit to which access is obtained by a slot in one of the rails. As far as the road bed is concerned, no new features are introduced beyond those with which the public are familiar. In the cable tramways of Highgate, Birmingham, and Edinburgh, we have become accustomed to the slot in the roadway, while in America this feature is very common. In the case before us the slot is not in the centre of the track, but replaces the groove in one of the rails, and therefore is less objectionable than in the cable system. The electrical advantages claimed for the series system, as compared with the parallel system of working tramways, is that a far smaller conductor is required to transmit the current with a given loss per mile. At Northfleet the current is kept constant at 50 ampères, and if there were a dozen cars on the line the current would not be increased. As each car was started the electromotive force at the terminals of the dynamo would be augmented by such a number of volts as multiplied by 50 ampères would represent the required power to drive that car on the particular part of the line on which it was travelling. A given size of conductor will suffice for any traffic that the line can carry. In determining its dimensions the questions to be considered are the highest electromotive force which it is advisable to employ, and the amount of power per mile which can be economically expended upon driving the current through the mains. There is a point for each special installation at which the interest on the cost of the conductor and the cost of power to force the current through the dead resistance of the main, are equal, and generally speaking this will mark the best section to adopt. The advantages of the series system are the greatest in long lines with heavy traffic. Under such circumstances the cost of copper mains on the parallel system becomes very heavy indeed, while if the traffic should increase beyond the original estimate of the designers the loss in the mains becomes ruinous. In America there are series tramways running very successfully in spite of their being erected with less care than is usual here. The spring contacts are said to give no trouble, and to last without renewal. Series working bears the same relation to parallel working in electric traction that the transformer system does to the direct supply system in electric lighting. All the electric lighting schemes now before the public provide for the use of transformers, either of the battery or of the converter type, and it is not surprising that the same principle should be coming to the front in tramways. The syndicate have done their work at Northfleet in first-rate style; everything is of the best and most substantial construction. We think that in their anxiety to show how small a conductor will do they have passed the economical limit, but possibly that was done designedly. The tramway managers who are to go to Northfleet to-day will certainly find much to interest them.

60. The road to Swanscombe is occupied by a lone tramcar which is captured on film towards the end of tramway operation. The track from Craylands Lane to the George and Dragon, Swanscombe only had a peak hour service. Make do and mend was the order of the day and car 14 has had a metal plate inserted at the base of the rocker panel in an attempt to strengthen the bodywork.
(National Tramway Museum)

61. There is plenty of time to stop and stare at the photographer who took this postcard view of The Hill, Northfleet in the early years of this century. The single tram track in the crown of the highway confirmed the tram's status as the most important road user at that time.
(R.Rosa Coll.)

Swanscombe to Denton.
Week Days.

Lenart George and Dragon.	Huggens' College.	Leather Bottle.	Rural Vale.	Public Hall.	Milton Place.	Arrive Denton.
P.M.	P.M.	P.M.	P.M.	P.M.	P.M.	P.M.
6 23	6 30	6 35	6 39	6 45	6 50	6 54
6 30	6 40	6 45	6 49	6 55	7 0	7 4
6 40	6 50	6 55	6 5	7 5	7 10	7 14
6 50	7 0	7 5	7 9	7 15	7 20	7 21
7 0	7 10	7 15	7 19	7 25	7 30	7 34
7 10	7 20	7 25	7 29	7 35	7 40	7 44
7 20	7 30	7 35	7 39	7 45	7 50	7 51
7 30	7 40	7 45	7 49	7 55	8 0	8 4
7 40	7 50	7 55	7 59	8 5	8 10	8 14
7 50	8 0	8 5	8 9	8 15	8 20	8 24
8 0	8 10	8 15	8 19	8 25	8 30	8 34
8 10	8 20	8 25	8 29	8 35	8 40	8 44
8 20	8 30	8 35	8 39	8 45	8 50	8 54
8 30	8 40	8 45	8 49	8 55	9 0	9 4
8 40	8 50	8 55	8 59	9 5	9 10	9 14
8 50	9 0	9 5	9 9	9 15	9 20	9 24
9 0	9 10	9 15	9 19	9 25	9 30	9 34
9 10	9 20	9 25	9 29	9 35	9 40	9 44
9 20	9 30	9 35	9 39	9 45	9 49	
9 30	9 40	9 45	9 49	9 55	9 59	
9 40	9 50	9 55	9 59	10 5	10 9	
9 50	10 0	10 5	10 9	10 15	10 19	
10 0	10 10	10 15	10 19	10 25	10 29	
10 12	10 22	10 27	10 31	10 37	10 41	
10 24	10 34	10 39	10 43	10 49	10 53	
10 36	10 46	10 51	10 55	11 1	11 5	
10 53	11 0	11 5	11 10	11 15	to Depôt.	
11 0	11 7	11 12				
11 12	11 19	11 24	} to Depôt			
11 24	11 31	11 36				
11 36	11 43	11 48				

62. This is how the artist at the Illustrated London News saw the electric traction experiments outside the Leather Bottel in 1889. The animated scene is further enhanced by the horse car. Whether the symbolism of the weary steed was intentional, we don't know, however, Dobbin had the last laugh as the new fangled Series Electrical Traction System quietly ground to a halt eighteen months later. (Illustrated London News.)

63. Four double deck, two horse trams were purchased by the Gravesend, Rosherville and Northfleet Tramways Co. in 1889. One of these cars is about to start its trot from the Leather Bottel into Gravesend. The two horses had an exciting life as, when the fire bell sounded, they were detached from the car and hitched to the fire engine. Passengers were then left stranded to await the outcome of the conflagration or they had to use Shanks's pony to complete their journeys! (J.H.Price Coll.)

64. The original fleet consisted of four, one horse, single deck cars and an open, cross-bench tram with seats for 22 people. A couple of the single deck trams had an afterlife on the Lincoln Tramways subsequent to arrival of the larger double deck cars at Gravesend. The trams were often in demand to carry trippers to Rosherville Gardens, part of an estate which opened in 1837 and contained a theatre, a refreshment room and a dance hall amongst its attractions. In 1910 the gardens finally closed, dereliction set in and the site was cleared and redeveloped in the 1920s. (R.Rosa Coll.)

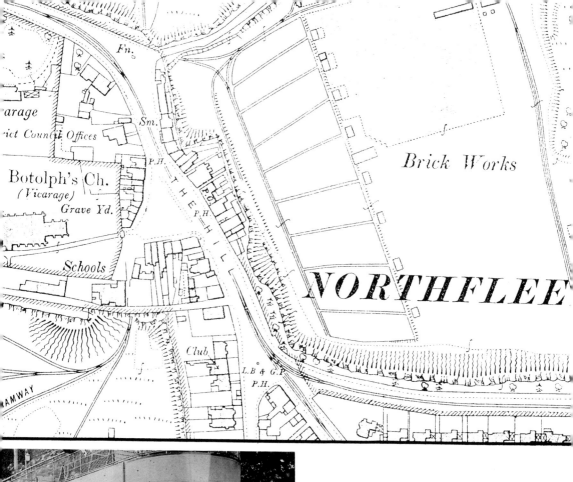

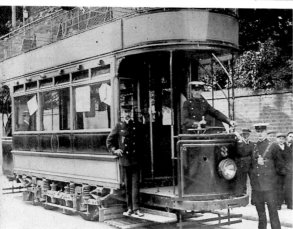

65. Car 3 was the second tram to bear this fleet number and it was acquired in 1905.
(R.Rosa Coll.)

66. A rather bedraggled and down-at-heel demi car 10 waits at the Leather Bottel around 1920/1; its working life is almost over.
(H.Lingwood Coll.)

Pelham Arms and Leather Bottle Route.

PELHAM ARMS TO LEATHER BOTTLE.				LEATHER BOTTLE AND PELHAM ARMS.			
a.m.	p.m.	p.m.	p.m.	a.m.	p.m.	p.m.	p.m.
9 0	12 15	3 30	6 45	9 8	12 23	3 38	6 53
9 15	12 30	3 45	7 0	9 23	12 38	3 53	7 8
9 30	12 45	4 0	7 15	9 38	12 53	4 8	7 23
9 45	1 0	4 15	7 30	9 53	1 8	4 23	7 38
10 0	1 15	4 30	7 45	10 8	1 23	4 38	7 53
10 15	1 30	4 45	8 0	10 23	1 38	4 53	8 8
10 30	1 45	5 0	8 15	10 38	1 53	5 8	8 23
10 45	2 0	5 15	8 30	10 43	2 8	5 23	8 38
11 0	2 15	5 30	8 45	11 8	2 23	5 38	8 53
11 15	2 30	5 45	9 0	11 23	2 38	5 53	9 8
11 30	2 45	6 0		11 38	2 53	6 8	
11 45	3 0	6 15		11 43	3 8	6 23	
12 0	3 15	6 30		12 8	3 23	6 38	

SATURDAYS.—Run as above until 11.15 p.m.
SUNDAYS.—Commence 10.0 a.m. and run as above until 10.30 p.m.

67. In contrast to the previous view, note the "as new" condition of car 9 in 1904. These trim, little vehicles seemed like the answer to the company's prayers. They were cheap to operate, only needing the services of one crewman, and they fed current back into the overhead by means of a regenerative control mechanism. These savings on fuel costs and wages were seen as the solution to the chronic deficits obtained on the Dover Road and Windmill Street sections.
(Tramway and Railway World)

GRAVESEND

St. James's Church to Pelham Arms Route—Week Days.

S. James's Church to Pelham Arms.			Pelham Arms to S. James's Church.		
A.M.	P.M.	P.M.	A.M.	P.M.	P.M.
8 8	4 8	8 53	8 0	4 0	8 45
8 23	4 23	9 0	8 15	4 15	8 53
8 38	4 38	9 8	8 30	4 30	9 0
8 53	4 53	9 15	8 45	4 45	9 8
9 8	5 8	9 23	9 0	5 0	9 15
9 23	5 15	9 30	9 15	5 8	9 23
9 38	5 23	9 38	9 30	5 15	9 30
9 53	5 30	9 45	9 45	5 23	9 38
10 8	5 38	9 53	10 0	5 30	9 45
10 23	5 45	10 0	10 15	5 38	9 53
10 38	5 53	10 8	10 30	5 45	10 0
10 53	6 0	10 15	10 45	5 53	10 8
11 8	6 8	10 23	11 0	6 0	10 15
11 23	6 15	10 30	11 15	6 8	10 23
11 38	6 23	10 38	11 30	6 15	10 30
11 53	6 30	10 45	11 45	6 23	10 38
P.M.	6 38	10 53	P.M.	6 30	10 45
12 8	6 45	11 0	12 0	6 38	10 53
12 23	6 53	11 15	12 15	6 45	11 8
12 38	7 0		12 30	6 53	
12 53	7 8		12 45	7 0	
1 8	7 15		1 0	7 8	
1 23	7 23		1 15	7 15	
1 38	7 30		1 30	7 23	
1 53	7 38		1 45	7 30	
2 8	7 53		2 0	7 38	
2 23	8 0		2 15	7 45	
2 38	8 8		2 30	7 53	
2 53	8 15		2 45	8 0	
3 8	8 23		3 0	8 15	
3 23	8 30		3 15	8 23	
3 38	8 38		3 30	8 30	
3 53	8 45		3 45	8 38	

SUNDAYS.—Commence 10.0 a.m. and runs every 15 mins. until 5 p.m., then as above until 10.30 p.m.

Ca 2482

GRAVESEND & NORTHFLEET ELECTRIC TRAMWAYS, LTD.

Denton	This Ticket is issued subject to the Co's Bye-laws and in exchange for the Workman's Return Ticket	Rural Vale
Milton Place		Factory Road
High Street		Huggens College
	Workman's Exchange	
Burch Rd		Swanscombe
Rotherville Church	and is available to the stage point punched.	Pelham Arms

68. On the Pelham Road branch, bogie car 7 works the service from Gravesend, St. James's Church to the Pelham Arms. It is passing a horse drawn water cart employed by the council to keep the dust down. (A.J. Watkins Coll.)

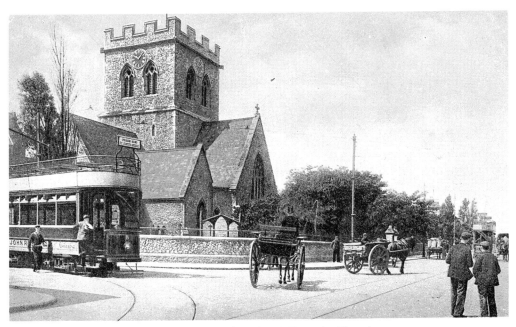

69. At the terminus by St.James's Church, a large eight wheel tram on the Pelham Road service waits for passengers. Pictures of these vehicles in the period before 1906 are very uncommon. (J.H.Price Coll.)

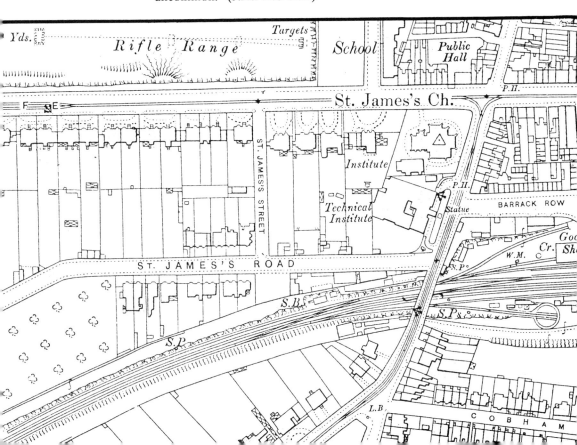

70. Looking along the main route, we are very fortunate to catch a glimpse of single deck car 8, which was bought from Taunton in 1921 and only had eight years service in Gravesend. (A.J.Watkins Coll.)

71. The triangular junction leading to New Road from the corner of Darnley Road can be seen in this picture taken early on in the life of the electric tramways. The neat arrangement of the overhead wires maintained them over the centre of the tramway. As the trams were first equipped with fixed head trolleys which allowed very little lateral movement, the wiring could not be strung from bracket arms at the side of the road. This was the more usual arrangement on systems using the swivel head collection method. (R.Rosa Coll.)

72. The motorman of car 11 has got down from
the driver's platform to sort something out as
he waits in the passing Loop along New Road.
(R.J.Harley Coll.)

73. Car 17, which we shall meet again shortly, heads into King Street, whilst demi car 10 waits at the terminus of the Windmill Street route. (A.J.Watkins Coll.)

74. We descend to ground level just in time to witness the departure of car 10 for the Old Prince of Orange. The driver cum conductor has turned the trolley pole and he is about to walk through the saloon to take up his post at the front of the car. (A.J.Watkins Coll.)

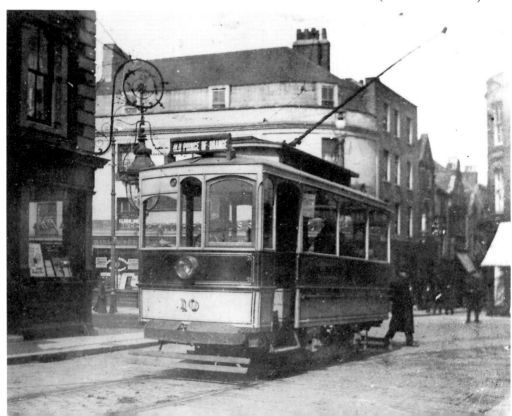

75. Views of double deck operation along Windmill Street are very rare. This photographic treasure bears the postmark 26th September 1906. (R.Rosa Coll.)

Windmill Street Route.
Week Days.

Leaves Bank at			Leaves Old Prince of Orange at		
a.m.	p.m.	p.m.	a.m.	p.m.	p.m.
8 23	1 53	6 30	8 36	2 8	6 38
8 45	2 0	6 38	8 53	2 15	6 45
9 0	2 8	6 45	9 8	2 23	6 53
9 15	2 15	6 53	9 23	2 30	7 0
9 30	2 23	7 0	9 38	2 38	7 8
9 45	2 30	7 8	9 53	2 45	7 15
10 0	2 38	7 15	10 8	2 53	7 23
10 15	2 45	7 23	10 23	3 0	7 30
10 30	2 53	7 30	10 38	3 8	7 38
10 38	3 0	7 38	10 45	3 15	7 45
10 45	3 8	7 45	10 53	3 23	7 53
10 53	3 15	7 53	11 8	3 30	8 0
11 0	3 23	8 0	11 15	3 38	8 8
11 8	3 30	8 8	11 23	3 45	8 15
11 15	3 38	8 15	11 30	3 53	8 23
11 23	3 45	8 23	11 38	4 0	8 30
11 30	3 53	8 30	11 45	4 8	8 38
11 38	4 0	8 38	11 53	4 15	8 45
11 45	4 8	8 45	p.m.	4 23	8 53
11 53	4 15	8 53	12 0	4 30	9 0
p.m.	4 23	9 0	12 8	4 38	9 8
12 0	4 30	9 8	12 15	4 45	9 15
12 8	4 38	9 23	12 23	4 53	9 30
12 15	4 45	9 30	12 30	5 0	9 38
12 23	4 53	9 38	12 38	5 8	9 45
12 30	5 0	9 45	12 45	5 15	9 53
12 38	5 8	10 0	12 53	5 23	10 8
12 45	5 15	10 15	1 0	5 30	10 23
12 53	5 23	10 30	1 8	5 38	10 38
1 0	5 30	10 45	1 15	5 45	10 53
1 8	5 38	11 0	1 23	5 53	11 8
1 15	5 45	11 15	1 30	6 0	11 23
1 23	5 53		1 38	6 8	
1 30	6 0		1 45	6 15	
1 38	6 8		1 53	6 23	
1 45	6 15		2 0	6 30	

SUNDAYS.—Commence at 10.8 a.m. and run every 15 minutes until 5 p.m., then run as above until 10.30 p.m.

76. At the end of the Windmill Street line, car 9 waits in 1904 whilst on a trial run. The fare for this shuttle service was one halfpenny; this was later raised to three farthings (three quarters of an old penny). Those readers who were brought up on the post- 1971 decimal currency may find it difficult to imagine such minute amounts! Since most passengers offered a penny coin for their ride, the driver either gave a farthing in change or a packet of pins in lieu, this was a common practice in those far off days.
(Tramway and Railway World)

77. We see a panorama of the terminus with the Old Prince of Orange Inn behind the one man operated tramcar. (R.Rosa Coll.)

FARES.

To or from	Fare.	Colour of Ticket.
High St., Gravesend and Old Prince of Orange		
St. James's Church and Pelham Arms..	$\frac{1}{2}$d	White
Pelham Arms and Leather Bottle..		
Denton and Public Hall, Gravesend		
Milton Place and Rural Vale ..		
Public Hall, Gravesend and Leather Bottle ..	1d	White
Rural Vale and Huggens' College		
Leather Bottle and Plough Pond		
Huggens' College and George and Dragon		
Black Eagle and Swanscombe Cross		
Denton and Rural Vale ..		Green
Milton Place and Leather Bottle	$1\frac{1}{2}$d	
Public Hall, Gravesend and Huggens' College		
Huggens' College and Swanscombe Cross ..		
Denton and Leather Bottle		
Milton Place and Plough Pond ..	2d	Pink
Rural Vale and Swanscombe		
Denton to Huggens' College		Yellow
High Street, Gravesend to George & Dragon ..	$2\frac{1}{2}$d	
Denton and Swanscombe ..	3d	Blue

Special Fares for Children under 12 years of age.

Denton, Gravesend, and Huggens' College ..	1d	White with red letter C.
Denton, Gravesend, and Swanscombe ..	$1\frac{1}{2}$d	White with Blue letter C

All Children, except Infants in arms, must be paid for.
Passengers are respectfully requested to observe that the Conductor punches, in their presence, a Ticket in the Section to be travelled over, and representing the value of the Fare paid.
Tickets are only available for the journey, and on the Car on which issued.
Whilst on the Car, passengers should retain their Tickets for inspection by the Company's Officials, or give them up on demand if required.

PLACES OF AMUSEMENT AND RECREATION.

▼▼▼▼▼▼▼▼▼▼▼▼▼▼▼▼▼▼

ROSHERVILLE GARDENS

(*Prettiest Gardens in the World*).
Electric Trams pass entrance every few minutes.

GRAVESEND PROMENADE
AND
RECREATION GROUND.

Alight from Electric Tram at Trinity Church.

. . WINDMILL HILL . .

The prettiest view in Kent is to be seen from this well-known Resort.
Electric Trams pass the entrance every few minutes.

Grand Theatre of Varieties.

2 Performances Nightly, 6.45 and 8.45.
Alight at Clock Tower, Gravesend, 1 minute's walk to Theatre.

PUBLIC HALL,
New Road, Gravesend.
Various Entertainments are held in this Hall.
Electric Trams pass the entrance every few minutes.

PUBLIC LIBRARY
AND
Municipal Technical Buildings,
Darnley Road, Gravesend.
Electric Trams pass the entrance every few minutes.

All visitors should avail themselves of a ride on the Electric Trams, and view the Cliffs and other scenes of Kent.

78. Our return to the centre of town is marked by the passing of car 16, still beautifully turned out with no trace of disfiguring advertisements. (R.J.Harley Coll.)

79. The driver of a double deck horse car turns round to observe a number of suspicious characters with sacks boarding his tramcar, in this 1900 view. (A.J.Watkins Coll.)

80. Car 17 is in its final state, fitted with a top cover. Bus competition looms behind the tram as Gravesend High Street braces itself for the imminent invasion of the internal combustion engine. (R.J.Harley Coll.)

81. We continue to follow the fortunes of car 17, seen here in near original condition. Our destination is displayed on the car, DENTON VIA LONDON RD. (R.Rosa Coll.)

TRAMCARS.
GRAVESEND and District

Gravesend and Northfleet Electric Tramways

No. of Tramcars : 18.

Principal Towns.				Population.
GRAVESEND	..	..	..	31,000
NORTHFLEET	..	..	..	16,000

Length of Track, $\left.\begin{array}{l} 3.90 \text{ Single} \\ 2.57 \text{ Double} \end{array}\right\} = 6.47$ Miles.

			Car Mileage.	Passengers Carried.
1922	..	..	378,299	3,887,263
1923	..	..	388,834	4,139,833
1924	..	..	429,506	4,372,297
Total for 3 years	..		1,196,639	12,399,393
Average	..		398,879	4,133,131

82. This photo completes the trio of car 17 views. The location is Gravesend Clock Tower; note the furniture delivery wagon to the left of the tram. (J.H.Price Coll.)

83. The same spot as the previous view, only this time the furniture wagon has returned empty. (R.J.Harley Coll.)

ton Road & Clock Tower, Gravesend.

84. Car 15 carries the emphatic message MILTON PLACE ONLY on the indicator blind. The Clock Tower was constructed for Queen Victoria's Jubilee and it was opened on 5th June 1888. (R.J.Harley Coll.)

85. Those people who think despicable acts of vandalism are a modern occurrence, might like to ponder the fact that Milton Parish Church, depicted here next to car 18, was stripped of the lead on its roof by thieves in 1790. It then took two years to reinstate the canopy over the congregation! A somewhat calmer situation reigns on this summer's day as the children play and the tram comes in sight of the terminus. (R.Rosa Coll.)

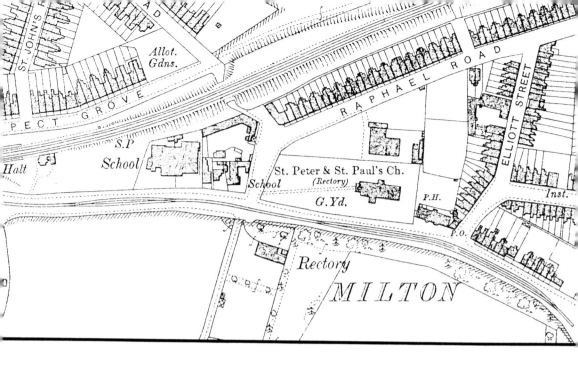

86. Denton Post Office marked the end of the line and the crew pause for a local photographer. There were plans to extend the tramways to Rochester, but gauge problems at Strood, where the standard Gravesend lines would have met the narrow (3ft. 6ins.) Chatham system, would have required a change of vehicle. (R.Rosa Coll.)

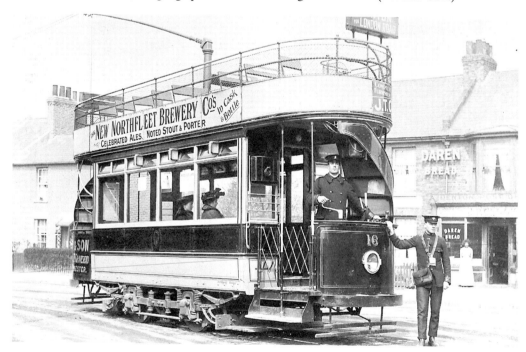

ROLLING STOCK

Cars 1 - 10. These were supplied in 1902 and were long eight wheel cars on Brill 22E maximum traction bogies, fitted with the pony wheel leading in the reversed position. They seated 34 inside and 33 on the top deck; they were equipped with fixed head trolleys. They were soon found to be unsuitable for Gravesend and were transferred to other undertakings in the BET group around 1905/6. Two cars went to Jarrow, four to Swansea and the remaining four to the South Metropolitan Electric Tramways at Croydon.

Cars 11 - 20. These were four wheel versions of the larger bogie cars; they were also built at Preston and were supplied in 1902. Seating was for 22 inside and 26 outside, and during the early 1920s cars 15 - 20 were fitted with top covers built locally by Beadle Brothers of Dartford. Since there were no railway bridges over the Gravesend tramways, the car roofs were not pitched as low as on other systems, this allowed plenty of headroom for top deck passengers. Cars on the Pelham Road route carried a green lamp at the stairhead. They rode on Brill 21E trucks of 6ft. wheelbase.

Replacement vehicles

Cars 1 -4. These were standard Brush built three window open top cars on Brush Aa type 6ft. wheelbase trucks.They were supplied in 1905 and seated 22 inside and 26 outside.They survived until the end in 1929 when they were sold for £5 each from the depot yard.

Cars 5 - 6. Basically very similar to the previous batch of trams, these two cars were purchased from Jarrow in 1908.

Cars 7 - 8. These were purchased secondhand from Taunton in 1921. Their 6ft. wheelbase trucks were converted to standard gauge and car 7 had the platforms altered for one man operation. Car 8 retained normal platforms and had the headlight on the dash. Further details of these trams can be found in the Middleton Press album *Exeter and Taunton Tramways.*

Cars 9 - 10. These were two Raworth Patent demi cars, supplied in 1904 on 5ft. 6ins. wheelbase trucks. They were fully enclosed and the driving platforms were equipped with vertical handbrake wheels. They were scrapped around 1921.

Livery of the Gravesend trams was originally maroon and cream, but in 1921 cars were repainted in brighter colours of cherry red and ivory.

87. Car 10 seen in original condition after delivery in 1902. (J.H.Price Coll.)

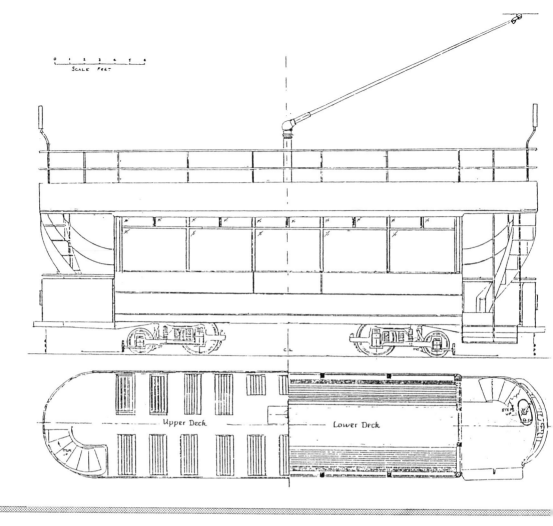

SCALE FEET

Upper Deck   Lower Deck

88. The inside of the lower saloon of one of the bogie cars illustrates the polished woodwork of the interior and the two long bench seats. (SMET official photo)

89. Car 34 (formerly of the Gravesend 1-10 batch) seen in SMET days, but still substantially in original condition.
(SMET official photo)

90. An end on view of one of the reversed stair cars shows many details of the car and contemporary staff uniforms in this restored photograph. (R.Rosa Coll.)

91. Car 18 is pictured in top covered condition with metal plate body strenthening in place above the truck. These cars carried no indicator boxes on the top deck, instead they had advertisement plates in yellow with black lettering. (H.Nicol)

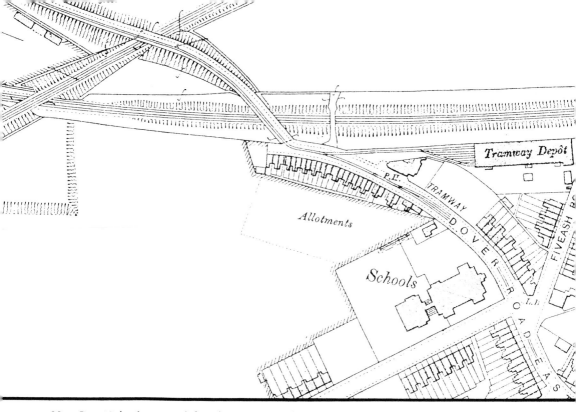

92. Car 12 is decorated for the Gravesend Carnival and underneath the bunting bears the new brighter cherry red and ivory livery with the BET wheel and magnet symbol on the waist panel. (A.J.Watkins Coll.)

93. Car 1 of the replacement batch, sporting all over advertising for Russell's Brewery Shrimp Brand beers and spirits. (R.Rosa Coll.)

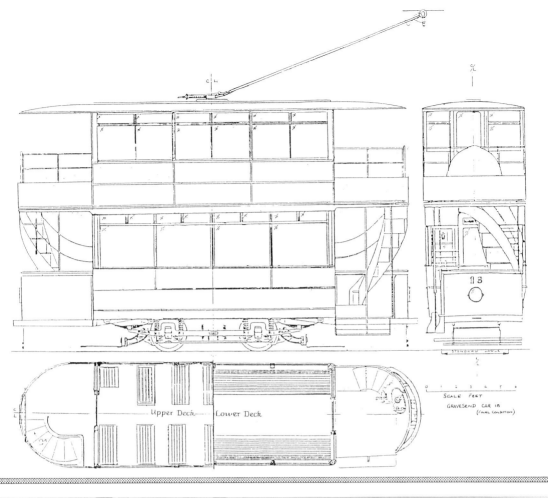

Upper Deck   Lower Deck

SCALE FEET
GRAVESEND CAR 18
(FINAL CONDITION)

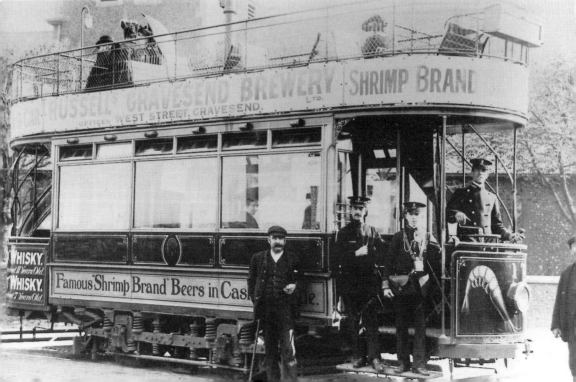

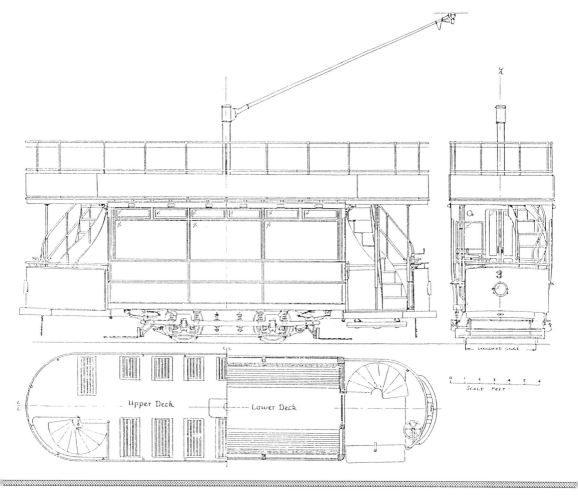

Upper Deck

Lower Deck

STANDARD GAUGE

SCALE FEET

94. Car 7, ex-Taunton, has been converted to one man operation. The route board reads LEATHER BOTTEL & DOVER RD. SCHOOLS. (H.Nicol)

95. Demi car 9 is pictured shortly after delivery. Note the anti-climbing plates on the fender and the motorman who is grasping the vertical handrake wheel. (R.J.Harley Coll.)

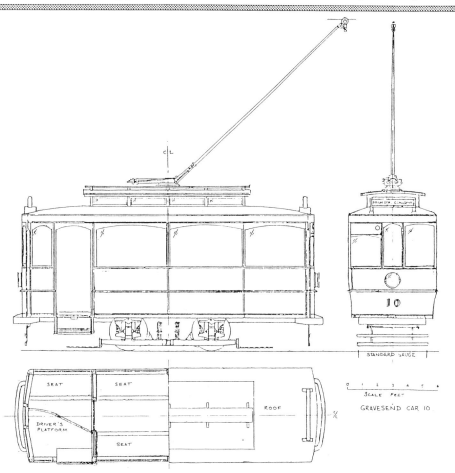

STANDARD GAUGE

SCALE FEET

GRAVESEND CAR 10

SEAT
SEAT
DRIVER'S PLATFORM
SEAT
ROOF

3. Sheerness Tramways

GEOGRAPHICAL SETTING

The Isle of Sheppey lies off the north coast of the county of Kent and is separated from the mainland by the narrow channel of the Swale. Sheerness is a coastal town on the Thames Estuary and the ground is reasonably level in the vicinity; there were no appreciable gradients for the trams to climb.

All maps are to 25" to 1 mile scale and are from the 1908 edition.

HISTORICAL BACKGROUND

Sheerness is known as a port and a naval establishment. King Charles II built a fort in the locality and later on dockyards were established; it was here that the body of Admiral Nelson was landed after the Battle of Trafalgar. Construction of a larger dockyard began in 1814 and in 1860 this facility was connected by railway to the main line at Sittingbourne. The other railway on the island, the Sheppey Light Railway, opened from Queenborough to Leysdown in 1901, but was closed due to lack of traffic, in 1950. The branch line to Sheerness was electrified in 1959 and is still in existence; all the island's lines are described fully in the Middleton Press volume *Branch Lines around Sheerness.*

The area attracted the attention of the British Electric Traction Company and construction of a small tramway system commenced in 1902, with the opening to the public the following year on 9th April. Sheerness Tramways were unusual in using bow collectors fitted to traditional British open top trams. The total overhead installation was acquired from Siemens in Germany and it has been suggested that the BET used Sheerness as test bed to try out a "continental" approach to small town tramways. The original 1902 order for twelve trams proved over optimistic for the passenger demands of the town, and four vehicles were sold to other tramways. The initial two services were:

Sheerness Pier to Sheerness East Station, via Town Station, Clock Tower and Monkey Farm.
Sheerness Pier to Cheyney Rock, via Town Station, Clock Tower and Broadway.

The through service to Cheyney Rock was short lived and a shuttle car was employed after 1904 to go back and forth from the Clock Tower.The BET also used the local tramways to train managers and engineers before they moved on to larger operations, and around seven individuals had the dubious honour of holding the managerial reins during the short life of the undertaking.The existence of electric traction on the streets was indeed short, and Sheerness became the first British tramway system to close down completely. There were various reasons for this early demise. Spare parts from Siemens became unobtainable due to the embargo on German goods during the First World War; bus competition became intense and the tramway had no funds for track renewals or new lines. The BET decided to cut its losses with the cessation of all service on 7th July 1917. The final irony was that the track and the Siemens overhead equipment were later removed by German prisoners of war.

SHEERNESS

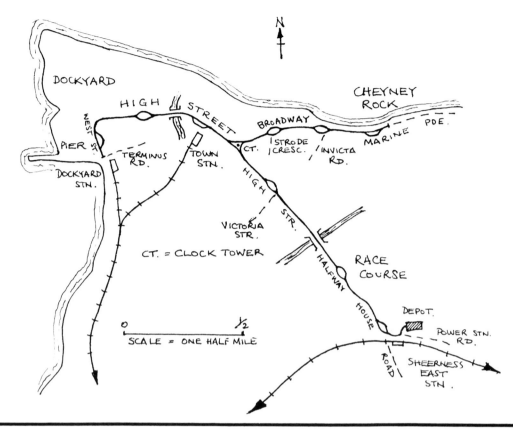

Map labels:
DOCKYARD
CHEYNEY ROCK
HIGH STREET
BROADWAY
WEST ST.
PIER ST.
STRODE CRESC.
INVICTA RD.
MARINE PDE.
CT.
DOCKYARD STN.
TERMINUS RD.
TOWN STN.
HIGH STR.
VICTORIA STR.
CT. = CLOCK TOWER
RACE COURSE
HALFWAY HOUSE
DEPOT
POWER STN. RD.
ROAD
SHEERNESS EAST STN.

0   ½
SCALE = ONE HALF MILE

96. A traveller arriving in Sheerness in Edwardian times would probably have alighted at Sheerness Town Station to be greeted by the sight of a lone tramcar negotiating the passing loop outside the station forecourt. (A.J.Watkins Coll.)

97. Further arrivals, in the shape of the military, make a detour round the stationary tram which is acting as a convenient grandstand to watch the marching ranks of soldiers. (R.Rosa Coll.)

98. This was a rare sight for the town, a convoy of two cars, seen here crossing the moat laid out as a defensive measure in the Napoleonic wars. Unfortunately passenger loadings did not come up to expectations and there are only a couple of individuals on each car in this postcard view. (R.Rosa Coll.)

99. The conductor on car 4 turns round just before the tram sets off in the direction of the Clock Tower. The track along the High Street was positioned next to the kerb. (J.H.Price Coll.)

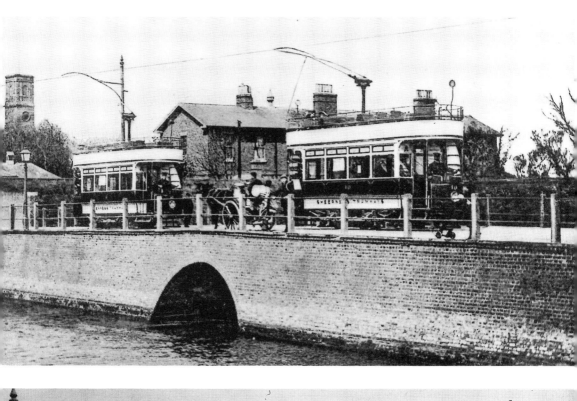

100. Car 4 is travelling along the High Street with Mr.Cutbush, the General Manager of the undertaking, at the controls. This was probably a trial run early in 1903, before the system opened to the public. (R.Rosa Coll.)

101. Clearances are checked by tramway officials as newly delivered car 7 edges its way towards the Clock Tower. (A.J.Watkins Coll.)

The Crescent, Sheerness-on-Sea.

102. The Clock Tower was built to commemorate the coronation of King Edward VII and Queen Alexandra in 1902. It was the focal point of the tramways in the centre of a triangular arrangement of tracks. The gent in the top hat to the right of car 1 is a reminder that the clothes one wore reflected social status in those far off days. (R.Rosa Coll.)

103. Another picture taken during a driver training session, shows a tram on the curve from Edward Street, Broadway into High Street. (R.Rosa Coll.)

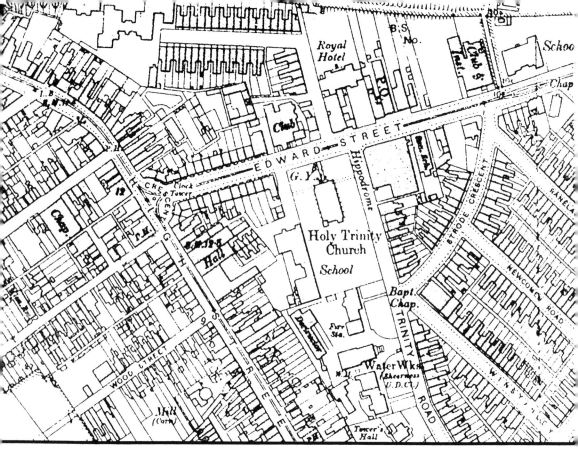

104. Car1 is the Cheyney Rock shuttle tram and has been provided with a route board by the lower saloon windows. The driver would have operated this car by himself; passengers had to board and alight by the driving platform, since the rear door was locked and the staircase was also blocked off. The motorman collected the fares as each passenger alighted from the tram. (R.J.Harley Coll.)

105. Around the year 1910, a fare stage number was fixed to selected traction standards; this was part of the BET "Fair Fare" scheme. In Sheerness the amount the passenger had to pay for four stages was one penny, for five stages a penny farthing, and for six stages tuppence (2d. or less than 1p...this was the maximum fare!). (R.Rosa Coll.)

106. We now set out to explore the Cheyney Rock route and car 10 waits to transport us along Broadway to the sea front esplanade. (A.J.Watkins Coll.)

107. The long, green painted bracket arms for the overhead wires stand out in the sunshine as the approaching tram passes the Conservative Club in Broadway. (R.Rosa Coll.)

108. Looking eastwards car 7 has just passed the grounds of Holy Trinity Church, built in 1836. The Tower behind the tram belongs to the Hippodrome, now also long gone. (R.Rosa Coll.)

109. There is time for some to stop and have a chat by the roadside, as car 4 trundles past with very few passengers on board. (R.J.Harley Coll.)

110. We cast a last glance back towards the distant Clock Tower whilst we wait at the passing loop for a tram to arrive. The track-work here was superfluous to requirements as only one tram worked this section, however, probably there were not enough funds to take out the points and insert a single line. (J.H.Price Coll.)

111. Car 3 pauses outside the Council Schools in Broadway, the children inside have no doubt got used to the sound of the trams outside their classrooms. Sunday School parties would often hire a special to take them out to the fields near the depot at Sheerness East; this was one of the few occasions a Sheerness tram would transport a full load of passengers. (R.Rosa Coll.)

112. In the days before exotic foreign holidays, many folk preferred to spend their meagre leisure hours contemplating the North Sea here on the Esplanade at Sheerness. If the stroll along the front was too much, there was always the tramcar for an unhurried return to the station and the train home. (J.H.Price Coll.)

113. A wonderful evocation of Edwardian life is presented in this view near Cheyney Rock terminus. Car 1 is about to make the journey back to town, on the side is an advertisement for freehold plots of land, these could be had for as little as £5 each and £30 would buy a whole acre of building land. (R.Rosa Coll.)

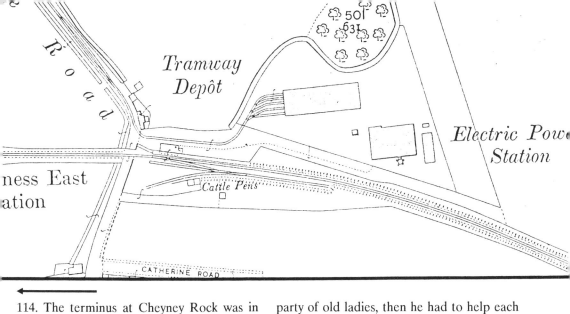

Map showing Tramway Depôt, Electric Power Station, Sheerness East Station, Cattle Pens, Catherine Road, with tree plots labelled 50' and 63'.

114. The terminus at Cheyney Rock was in Marine Parade and here car 1 waits at the last passing loop before the end of the track. It was normally the conductor's job to pull down the bow collector and swing it round to face the opposite direction when the tram reached the terminus. When this route was one man operated, a certain Driver Mills on reaching Cheyney Rock had to collect the fares from a party of old ladies, then he had to help each one off the car, finally his task was to change over the bow collector, lock the saloon doors, and put down the step at the opposite driving platform before setting off! He was reported for being ten minutes late and a fine was exacted by the company. For this work he received four pence ha'penny (2p) an hour! (R.Rosa Coll.)

115. The depot and power station were situated next to Sheerness East Station and this was the setting for the group photograph. (R.Cook Coll.)

116. Farewell to Sheerness Tramways. This is the wake laid on for the closure in 1917; note that the tram nearest the depot doors has already been partially dismantled. (R.Rosa Coll.)

ROLLING STOCK

Twelve trams were delivered to Sheerness in 1903, they were four wheel, open top cars, built by Brush at Loughborough, and mounted on Brush A type 6ft. wheelbase trucks. Four trams were quickly sold to another BET company, the City of Birmingham Tramways. These cars were subsequently transferred to the Birmingham and Midland Tramways.

Eight cars were retained at Sheerness until the end of the system in 1917, they were then sold to Darlington Corporation where they lasted until 1926.

The first Sheerness livery was maroon lake and cream; cars were later repainted dark green and cream.

117. Car 7 is in the original maroon and cream livery with the silver BET "wheel and magnet" device on the waist panel. (R.J.Harley Coll.)

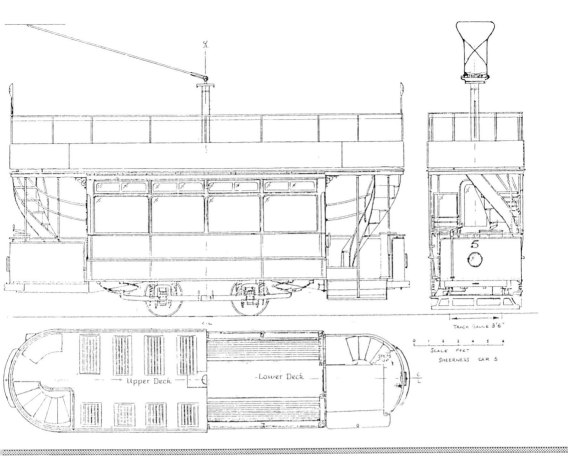

SHEERNESS CAR 5

118. Four Sheerness cars were acquired by the City of Birmingham Tramways in 1903, and one was later resold to the Devonport and District Tramways. Car 53 seen here, found a home with the Birmingham and Midland Tramways and was placed in the South Staffs. fleet of that company in 1911/12. The Siemens bow had been removed and a normal trolley standard substituted. (R.J.Harley Coll.)

119. The letters on the front of the 1925 petrol electric car confirm the ownership of Herne Bay Urban District Council. The track gauge was an odd three feet four and one half inches; the metric equivalent is 1029mm, so the mystery of this unusual track gauge remains. (R.Rosa Coll.)

4. Herne Bay Pier

HISTORICAL BACKGOUND

The resort of Herne Bay lies on the North Kent coast and a pier was built in the 1830s with a tramway running the length of the structure. Motive power was supplied by the prevaling wind which acted on a sail driven trolley. The first pier was dismantled in 1871 and a new pier, opened in 1873, was later equipped with an electric tramway which first ran in April 1899. A single Brush built, eight wheel, single deck tramcar entered service using the conduit method of current collection. In 1901 two ex-Bristol, open bench horse trams were purchased and one was attached to each end of the original tramcar thus making a three car "train" of vehicles. Also in 1901 the pier tramway suffered a rather nasty accident when one of the open cars derailed and plummeted into the sea; this resulted in one fatality. The pier was closed during the 1914-18 war and the tramway fleet sold off. In the 1920s a new petrol electric tram was commissioned and it shuttled up and down until 1934 when a more sophisticated battery electric car was purchased. All was well until the outbreak of the Second World War in 1939 when parts of the tramway and the pier were blown up as an anti-invasion measure. Thus Herne Bay's only tramway went out with a bang!.

120. Before we sail away from North Kent we get a final glimpse of the battery electric car with the old petrol electric tram dumped behind. Note the two mini platforms thoughfully provided for intending passengers.
(A.J.Watkins Coll.)